HAL•LEONARD®
VIOLIN PLAY-ALONG

AUDIO ACCESS INCLUDED

Cajun and Zydeco Songs

PLAYBACK+
Speed • Pitch • Balance • Loop

To access audio visit:
www.halleonard.com/mylibrary

"Enter Code"
5354-6068-2036-1062

ISBN 978-1-5400-8892-5

Jon Vriesacker, violin
Audio arrangements by Peter Deneff
Recorded and Produced by Jake Johnson
at Paradyme Productions

Visit Hal Leonard Online at
www.halleonard.com

Contact us:
Hal Leonard
7777 West Bluemound Road
Milwaukee, WI 53213
Email: info@halleonard.com

In Europe, contact:
Hal Leonard Europe Limited
42 Wigmore Street
Marylebone, London, W1U 2RN
Email: info@halleonardeurope.com

In Australia, contact:
Hal Leonard Australia Pty. Ltd.
4 Lentara Court
Cheltenham, Victoria, 3192 Australia
Email: info@halleonard.com.au

Iko Iko

Words and Music by Barbara Ann Hawkins, Joan Marie Johnson and Rosa Lee Hawkins

3

Jambalaya
(On the Bayou)

Words and Music by Hank Williams

Jolie Blonde

Cajun Folk Song

La Porte En Arrière
(The Back Door)
Words and Music by D.L. Menard

My Toot Toot

Words and Music by Sidney Simien

Ya Ya

Words and Music by Morris Levy and Clarence Lewis

Zydeco Gris Gris

Words and Music by Michael Doucet

When the Saints Go Marching In

Words by Katherine E. Purvis
Music by James M. Black